The Abecedarian Book

The Abecedarian Book

By Charles W. Ferguson

LITTLE, BROWN AND COMPANY

BOSTON · TORONTO

Published simultaneously in Canada
by Little, Brown & Company (Canada) Limited

PRINTED IN THE UNITED STATES OF AMERICA

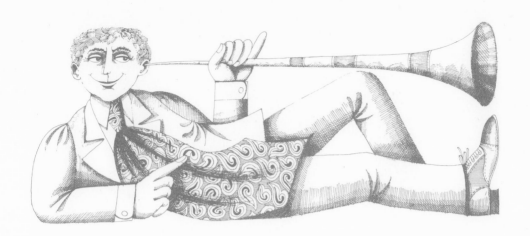

LISTEN!

Big words make nice noises. There are more sounds in hippopotamus than in cat, more in allegory than in tale. If you learn a small word you learn a small word and that is about all there is to it. But if you learn a big word you learn a dozen other words along with it because most big words are related to other words.

This is the reason for *The Abecedarian Book*. Abecedarian is a real word three hundred years old to describe a person who is either learning or teaching the ABC's. The book is made up of big words and it is to be read aloud, so that all the sounds of the big words become clear to the ear.

Big words are good to listen to. Some of them would be as long as verses if they were written in verse form:

> *Hip*
>> *po*
>>> *pot*
>>>> *a*
>>>>> *mus*

And it is fun to write words that way, just to give an idea of all the sounds in them. Take some of the words on the following pages and write or have someone write them in verse form and see how many sounds you hear. Remember what Lewis Carroll wrote: "Alice had not the slightest idea of what latitude was, or longitude either, but she thought they were nice grand words to say."

One reason you will get quite a few sounds is that big words have lots of vowels. Vowels give words sound and sound effects. They give words voices. Vowel is a word that comes from an old word, vocalis, meaning voice. Vowels are the letters a e i o u. Try taking those letters out of a big word (or any word) and see how little sound you have left.

Big words are built with blocks called syllables, a word that comes from two old words meaning to hold together. So syllables have stickum on them and they stick to other syllables. Hip is a syllable and so is po and they stick together. And that's the way it is with other big words. They string together like a long train. They go on and on — it's hard to know when to stop spelling Mississippi.

Another nice thing about syllables is that they often help you figure out what a big word means. Words live in families and they often have family resemblances. There is some feature of a word that reminds you of the family it comes from. It's the way it is when your parents say of a boy, "He looks like a Thompson." There is something about the curly hair or the shape of the nose that all the Thompson children have.

If you look up a word or have someone look it up for you, listen to all the syllables and note especially what the dictionary tells you about the meaning of each.

Well, anyway, it is fun to find meaning through sound, just as you often get the meaning of music through the sound of music.

Happy listening in the pages ahead!

The Abecedarian Book

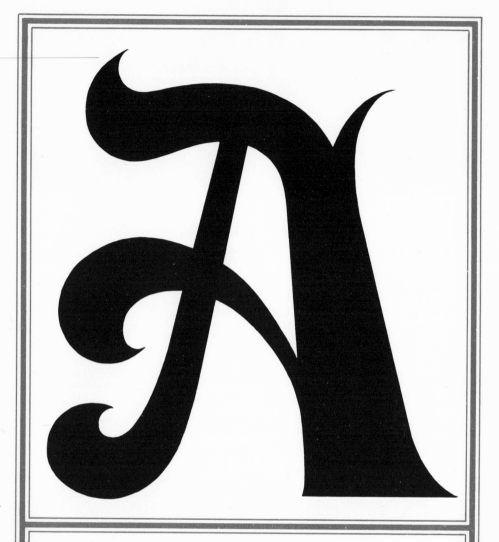

is for Antediluvian

A is for ANTEDILUVIAN

Of course you could just say "before the Flood," because that is what antediluvian means. But antediluvian, besides being a beautiful word with little bells ringing in it, is also a comical word. And if you learn the life story of the word and see how men have used it for its humor as well as for its loveliness, you will understand a great deal more than the word itself.

Antediluvian tells us, among other things, how our English-American language is made up of older languages. Rome was located in a country called Latium and Romans spoke a language called Latin. Roman legions carried Latin with them and left it wherever they went. They conquered what is now England and left their language there, so that when the English made up words, even centuries after the Romans had left, they often turned to Latin.

When they wanted a word to mean "before the Flood," when they wanted to say it all in one word, they took two Latin words and put them together. They took ante, which means before. Ante is a prefix — a fixed beginning of a word that you will find in many other words. You will hear it in anteroom, a small room you go into before you enter a big one. You will hear it in antebellum, which means before the war, bellum being the Latin word for war. And you'll find it in the letters you see written every day. A.M. stands for ante meridiem and it tells you of the morning, of the time before the sun reaches the meridian and is directly overhead.

The Latin word for flood is diluvium. You have heard a flood referred to as a deluge. The Flood in the word antediluvian is the one in which Noah took two of every beast, according to the Bible story, and kept them secure in his Ark. It was a turning point and starting-over point in the history of the Jews. It happened way, way back there, and anything that happened before the Flood was thought of as very, very old. It belonged to another time.

It is not surprising that by 1726 (or long before our American Revolution) men had started using the word antediluvian to mean a thing was out-of-date — so much out-of-date that it was comical. It was something unbelievably old. People would say that a tottering old man was antediluvian. Charles Lamb, the English essayist, spoke of "an antediluvian makeshift of a building."

The word still hangs on in our speech and you will hear it occasionally. This means that it serves a purpose, that there is a place for it. It's a nice word with a funny meaning and that's one way you will hear it. Today you hear people say to a fellow who does not have the latest car but insists on driving one that is behind the times, "Where did you get that antediluvian model?"

The word can be used in a more serious way. Benjamin Franklin, writing of the good things he saw ahead of his day and thinking how health might be improved, foresaw a time "when our lives might be lengthened beyond the antediluvian standard." It is also a word that can help draw pictures. S. J. Perelman, describing a night scene from a hut on stilts in the jungle, writes: "An amber spotlight simulating the full moon had been turned on, and it made the beasts seem even more antediluvian than normally." Here, as in *The Hunting of the Snark,* the word gives a creepy feeling:

There was silence supreme! Not a shriek, not a scream,
Scarcely even a howl or groan,

As the man they called "Ho" told his story of woe
In an antediluvian tone.

is for Bioluminescent

B is for BIOLUMINESCENT

The beauty of being a word detective is that if you keep your eyes and ears open, as every detective must, you can learn to use clues to find your way into and out of every big word. Clue is a word that can also be spelled clew, but however you spell it, it is the name for a ball of string. Once upon a time, in the tales the Greeks told about their gods, there was a mighty young warrior named Theseus who went into a deep cave with winding passages to slay a monster. Ariadne, a woman who loved him, gave Theseus a clue which he could unwind as he went along and then follow back to the entrance of the dark cave after he had slain the monster.

To find your way into and out of bioluminescent, begin with bio. The Greek word for life or living things was bios. Once you see bio in a word you know that the word has something to do with life or things that are alive. In biography, for example, bio combines with the Greek word graph, meaning write, and you have the written story of a man's life. Biology is a study of living things.

In bioluminescent you have two other words to guide you, words that you will find in other big words. One is lumin. It is from a Latin word meaning light. You will hear the word illuminated and know that it tells of something that is lighted. People will speak of poor illumination and you will know that they mean poor lighting. Or they may say that a thing is luminous and you know that it glows. It may have light in it and give off light. A lightning bug is luminous.

A lightning bug, in fact, is bioluminescent — because the light it gives off comes from the life in it. It isn't reflected. It comes, as the term escent tells us, from the fact of life itself. Escent is also Latin in origin and it means being, or starting to be. You will find it in other words, such as convalescent, a person who has been ill but is starting to get well or is in the process of getting well. An adolescent is a person who is starting to grow up or is in the process of growing up.

When a thing is bioluminescent, then, it is giving off light from the very act of living. Many tiny creatures of the sea give off light, so that when you stand at the rail of a ship at sea there are times when the waters are alight from the glow of these creatures. The sea itself looks bioluminescent.

Bio is a syllable you will see often. Sometimes it is buried in a word but you can fetch it out and at least have a clue. A warm and lovely word with bio buried in it is symbiosis. It describes the living together of two organisms in a way that is good for both. They may be two plants or an animal and a plant. There is a fungus (from the Greek word for sponge) that lives around the roots of certain forest trees. The fungus draws its food from the plant root and in turn feeds the plant and brings it water. Two things not alike live closely together and both gain by it.

Symbiosis is one of the unexpected marvels that come to light in a word. These marvels are all around us and often reveal themselves to us through words. Bioluminescent describes another. It tells us that there is not only life but also light in some of the world's tiniest creatures.

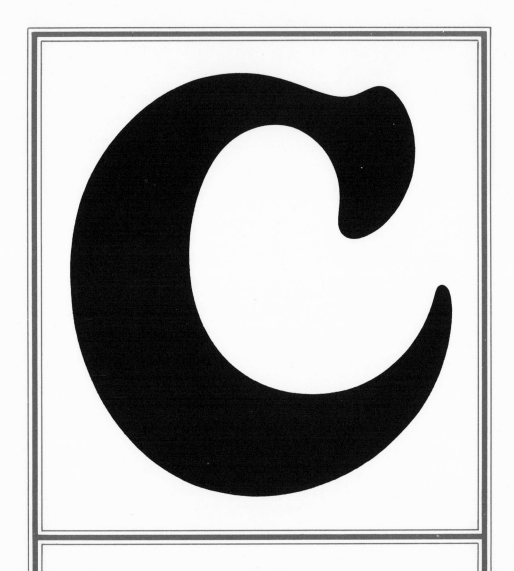

is for Cacophony

C is for CACOPHONY

Let us note first that phone is the Greek word for sound or voice. When Alexander Graham Bell in 1876 needed a word to describe the instrument he had invented, he adopted the term telephone, from the Greek words tele and phone. Tele means far off, so that telephone literally means a far-off sound or voice; with his invention the far-off voice was brought close by means of electrical impulses.

The same Greek word for voice is to be found in the word cacophony. Here it is combined with another Greek word, kakos, meaning bad, evil, or harsh. When you get a lot of bad noise without harmony or gentle sounds, you have cacophony. When your mother tells you to cut out the racket, she is talking about cacophony. No one objects to the laughter of children or to the pleasant noises they make when they play in a friendly way. It's the harsh and raucous and quarrelsome sound that makes cacophony.

Kakos in the form of caco will be found in other English words.

Your teacher may tell you that you have bad handwriting, that it looks as if your marks had been made by a chicken scratching the paper. This is cacography. Graph, as you know, is the Greek word for write. Or you may have a bad habit or two, an itch or a mania for doing something you have been told not to do. What you've got in that case is cacoethes. Ethos is the Greek word for custom or habit. If you don't watch your cacoethes the goblins will get you.

Remembering that phone is the Greek word for sound or voice, you will enjoy discovering it for yourself in other words. It's like an Easter egg hunt. A phonograph is an instrument that writes down or records the voice or music. There are two Greek words bobbing up at you again.

Sooner or later you are bound to hear your teacher talking about phonetics. There is nothing bumfuzzling about the word if you remember phone. Phonetics has to do with the way words sound and the way they can be remembered because of the way they sound. It suggests that we ought to hear the voice of words as well as remember their faces — just as you know voices on the phone as well as faces on the street.

If you spell a word phonetically, you spell it the way it sounds. Spelled phonetically, the word through would be spelled thru. Theodore Roosevelt, when he was President of the United States, started a movement for simplified spelling. Before you get thru with skool you may wish he had suckseeded. Then you wouldn't have to learn that rough is spelled the way it is instead of ruff.

So there are many sound effects in the word cacophony and it's hard to keep the mind on all of them. For while it is made up of a bad word at the beginning, it has a happy ending. And sometimes that is the way cacophony turns out. You hear a new piece of music and it annoys you, seems cacophonous. One critic who did not care for the German composer Richard Strauss spoke of him as a cacophonophilist — a man in love with unpleasant noises. You too may think that some composer is trying simply to use noises. Then you hear music a number of times and you begin to get the drift. You hear the real voice in it and it is not so bad. Before long it may be good.

P.S. stands for postscript. Post is the opposite of ante and script comes from the Latin term for writing. So a postscript is something added, usually to a letter.

In this case it is an afterthought and a slight warning, lest you think that all words that have phone in them have to do with the voice. One big exception is the word phony. It means cheap or false and some say it comes from the way people mispronounced a man's name.

The man's name was Forney. Forney was a man who made cheap rings and other pieces of jewelry. These were sold by street peddlers around 1902 in the United States. They were not much good but they looked like the real thing. In time this jewelry got to be called Forney jewelry. People overheard the word and did not take the pains to look into it or learn how it was pronounced. They simply said it the way it almost sounded, almost phonetically. It became phony.

Other students of words have a different story, but it has the same point. The Irish word for ring is fainne, pronounced fawney. It is said that Irish street swindlers of bygone days would pretend to find a ring they themselves had dropped. It would be covered with gold to look expensive. The swindler would offer to sell it to a passerby for a high price, claiming he offered a bargain. The person who bought it would later find that he had been gypped (this by the Irish and not the gypsies). The ring was false and the ring that was false came to be called a fawney. The spelling was changed by degrees to sound more the way it sounded to people who didn't know the origin.

So, in a funny way, even the word phony has some of the Greek word for sound in its story.

more
to
come

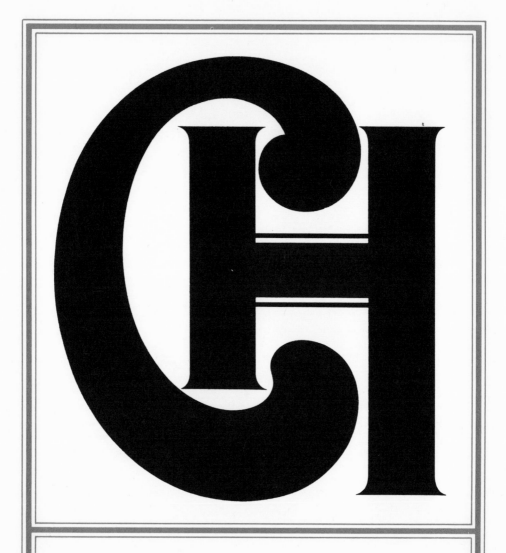

is for Characteristic

CH is for CHARACTERISTIC

The way ch is pronounced in this word tells you at a glance something about it. How could ch come to sound like k — as in character and Christmas and choir and chord? The answer is that these words came down to us as a part of the language we inherited from the Greeks.

So character is Greek in origin, and the word characteristic, made from it, is Greek in flavor, although of course a great many changes in language have gone on since days of the early Greeks. (The word change is pronounced the way it looks because it came from a cluster of languages and not from the Greek; if it had come from the Greek it would be pronounced kange.) The original Greek word that gives us our word character meant a tool or instrument for engraving, for making a strong, deep mark in stone or metal. It is interesting to see how this use of the word continues to this day. In a printing shop the letters and figures used are referred to as characters.

Outside printing and engraving the word character took on a

special meaning, but it had always to do with a distinctive mark. You have heard folks say that so-and-so is a character. This means that he stands out from the crowd, follows his own habits of dress and speech. By the same token, when a man has character, it means that he has strong marks. He is distinctive. He is not, as the Apostle Paul puts it, blown about by every wind of doctrine.

Characteristics are simply distinctive marks that show up character, that underline it, so to speak. But characteristics can apply to things as well as people. For instance, the dictionaries illustrate this point by referring to the characteristic smell of cabbage — and we know what they are talking about. They also speak of the characteristic taste of honey — and we know about that too. In both cases there is nothing else like these characteristics.

It is that way with people. When we speak of the characteristics of people we refer to the distinctive marks that the influences of parents and friends and teachers have left on them. They may be characteristically kind and we know what to expect of them. When things like this happen, we have a habit of saying that people are behaving in character. You can rely on their characteristics. And when someone surprises us by his action when we expect the best, we say that what he does is out of character.

It helps to keep in mind the Greek idea as well as the Greek word when we think of characteristics. Our character may be thought of as the sum total of our characteristics.

more
to
come

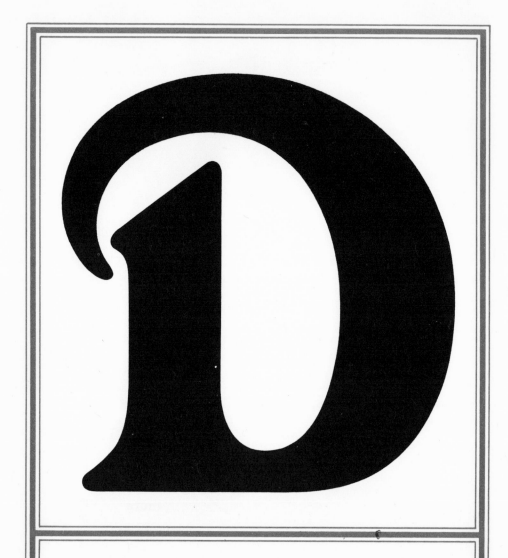

is for Diagnostician

D is for DIAGNOSTICIAN

A diagnostician is a doctor so skilled in sorting out the signs and symptoms of sick people that he may do nothing else. He may spend all his time finding out the cause of a pain and let other doctors treat it. He may do it himself, of course, but in either case the important thing is to detect, which means literally to take the cover off. A doctor must be sure of what is wrong before he can do right. No use treating you for appendicitis if you have mononucleosis.

Diagnosis is a much older word than diagnostician and thereby hangs a significant fact. Diagnosis has always been a part of the practice of medicine, naturally, and has become a specialty only in the past hundred years or so. The word diagnosis is made up quite simply by joining the prefix dia, meaning, in this case, apart or between, with gnosis, the Greek word for knowledge. Diagnosis is the name for the ability to know the difference between one cause and another.

Gnosis may turn up in other words. You may hear it said that a man is an agnostic. This means that he is a non-knower. He may make a business of not knowing or not claiming to know about such matters as the existence of God; or he may say that he hopes to know later. And the prefix dia in diagnosis you will find in other words, as in dialogue, where it combines with the Greek word for word, logos, to describe speech between two persons.

The most interesting and revealing part of diagnostician, however, is the suffix, ician. Suffix means literally to fasten underneath, but for all practical purposes it is a sound or syllable added to a word to change or broaden its meaning. Ician, which comes from the French, is a handy suffix in a good many ways. It tells of a person who is engaged in or specializes in some trade or profession. You find it in mathematician — a person whose field is mathematics; in rhetorician, rhetoric being from the Latin word for orator, a person whose special field is the study of speech.

Not infrequently people feel that they can lend dignity to what they are doing by adding the suffix ician to the name of the job. A person who runs a beauty parlor may be referred to as a beautician. A person whose business is the burial of the dead may refer to himself as a mortician, from the Latin word mors, for death, and the convenient suffix ician.

So the word diagnostician tells you about the development of fields of interest and about the way the language grows. A doctor who may not actually treat a patient (sufferer, from the Latin patiens) but may simply be skilled in finding causes and lets you know his specialty and the dignity of his position by the word diagnostician.

more
to
come

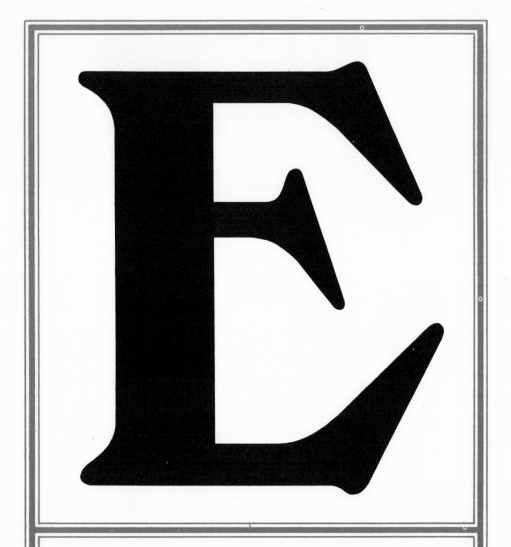

is for Encyclopedia

E is for ENCYCLOPEDIA

As everyone knows, you can learn something about almost everything in an encyclopedia. You can also learn many things from the
word itself. It is made up of other words that talk to each other,
and as you study them they tell a story of how parents feel about
their children and how through the years adults want to share
what they know.

The chief little word in the big word is cyclo. Cyclo is from
the Greek word for circle: kyklos. You can recognize cyclo in
words we use every day: in bicycle (having two wheels), tricycle
(having three wheels), motorcycle (a contraption with cycles or
wheels turned by a motor). You will find cyclo in the dreadful
word cyclone, which tells you of a storm that moves in a circle.
And you'll find it in those awful-looking giants of Greek my-
thology called Cyclops. These giants had only one eye and it was
very big and very round, right in the middle of the forehead.

In encyclopedia, cyclo describes a circle men have tried to draw
around knowledge. It goes all around and includes everything.

Or tries to. The wish of men to get all facts in one circle is very old. The first attempt we know about was made by a Roman named Pliny the Elder, who died A.D. 79. His *Natural History* was in thirty-seven volumes. It included as much as he could put together not only about science but about art and other things of his day.

Since Pliny men have been trying to keep information in a circle and make orbits around it. And one reason they have done it is that they want to share what they know with the mind that wants to know. For there is another important word besides cyclo. It is paideia, meaning education, and this in turn is drawn out of another Greek word — the most important of all. This is pais, meaning child.

So in origin as well as fact an encyclopedia is a thing to teach a child all about everything. It is a book for children in that men want to pass on what they have learned and keep it neat for others.

Of course what they have learned gets bigger and bigger all the time. One professor says our body of facts has doubled in the past fifty years and will double again in the next ten. So the task of drawing a circle around it gets harder and harder, and we now have special encyclopedias of this and that, encircling small fields of special information. And even they are getting big. There's no telling where it will all end. Perhaps in an encyclopedia of encyclopedias.

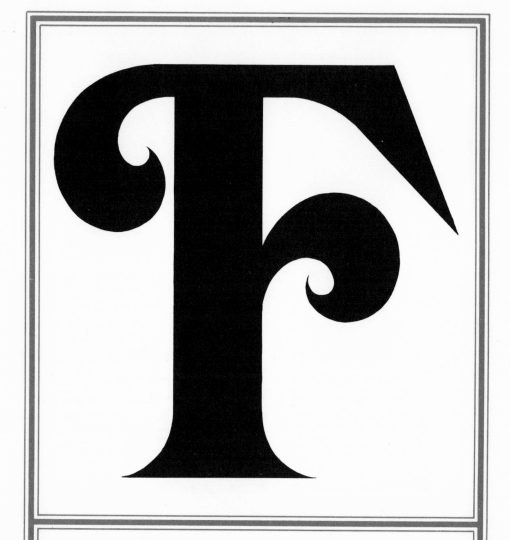

is for Flamboyancy

F is for FLAMBOYANCY

The next time you see a big truck loaded with gasoline or compressed gas, you may see painted on the back end of it the word flammable. It may be spelled with only one m. But however it is spelled, it will be the Latin word flamma put to modern use. Flamma is flame in our language, and when flammable appears on the back of a truck it warns that what the truck carries could be set on fire. You will notice also that the truck has a chain dragging on the pavement. This is to drain off any electricity or sparks that might set the truck on fire.

Flamma is the basis of a number of English words we see and use and hear people use, including flamboyant. When a thing is flamboyant it resembles a flame in some way. A certain kind of architecture in the fifteenth and sixteenth centuries was said to be flamboyant because it had tracery around the windows that looked like flames. Flamboyant is a French word transferred to English and sometimes it is used to tell us that an object is the color of flame, a very bright hue. It is even applied to the way people talk. If they use flowery or florid language and exaggerate a great deal and try to color their speech, they are showing flamboyancy.

A word closely related to flamboyancy is flambeau. It came first, in fact, and tells us something of the way houses were lighted in the Middle Ages. A large candle or torch would be set in a holder on the wall. It burned brightly against the wall. The flames danced in the draftiness of the old castles and certainly gave people a chance to describe the fire in the flambeau as flamboyant. You get some idea of the rambunctious manners of the period when houses were lighted with these torches from a line by Dryden: "The king seized a flambeau with zeal to destroy."

Another word associated with flamma is flamingo, a bird of brilliant color, looking almost as if it were on fire. And not too long ago there was a slang use of the world flame. A young man might speak of the girl he felt warmly about at the moment as his flame. If he had referred to her as his current but transient inamorata, he would have been speaking flamboyantly.

You may be amused to know that the longest word in the Oxford English Dictionary begins with an f. It is floccinaucinihilipilification. It describes the habit we all have of considering something worthless if we don't understand it or want it. This sesquipedalian word was made up in the early 1700's to look and sound as funny as it does. It is simply a string of Latin terms, flocci, nihili, nauci and pili, all of which are words for saying that a thing amounts to little or nothing.

The man who made up floccinaucinihilipilification probably got a great kick out of it, especially when he saw that others were using it and it might get into the language to entertain people for generations to come. Making up words can be a fine pastime. Gelett Burgess, an American essayist, once made his own dictionary and called it *Burgess Unabridged*.

He made up six hundred words that he thought the English language needed in spite of the six hundred thousand it already had. One of his words, blurb, meaning to talk like a publisher, got into the regular dictionaries and you will find it credited to him.

In the same book Burgess coined (as we say) the word huzzlecoo to mean a heart-to-heart talk. It's a nice word and if you like it you can have it. If you and your friends use it enough and some writer picks it up and it begins to appear in print, huzzlecoo may get into the dictionaries yet.

Or you can make up your own word for huzzlecoo and see if it will be accepted. Just be sure it is characteristic of what it describes and not too flamboyant.

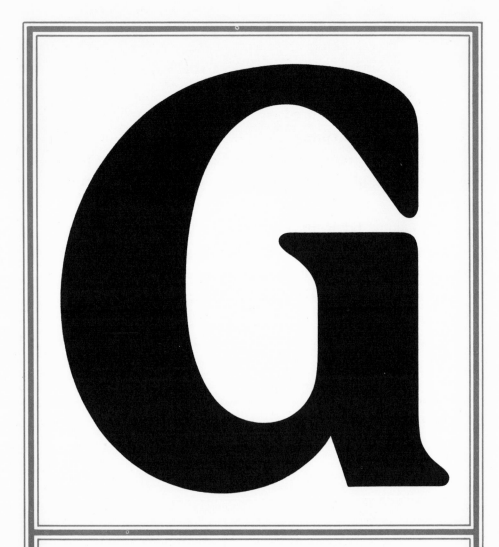

is for Gerrymander

G is for GERRYMANDER

This is one of those words that have a man's name in them. There are many. Your milk is pasteurized. It has been put through a process worked out by a great French chemist, Louis Pasteur, who died in 1895. Pasteur found a way to make milk pure by heating it to a temperature of 142 degrees Fahrenheit for thirty minutes. This kills any harmful germs in it but does not destroy the food value.

Well, G is for gerrymander. Mr. Elbridge Gerry, whose last name makes the first part of the word, found a way of drawing lines on a map to give his political party a big advantage in an election. It happened in 1812, when Mr. Gerry was governor of Massachusetts. He wanted to be sure of having a majority of his party in the senate or upper house of the state legislature. Senators were elected from districts. Governor Gerry caused a bill to be passed by the legislature that changed the lines of the state's election districts in a way that might favor his party. Although the Gerry party's candidates for senator did not get as many votes as those of the other party in the state election of 1812, it ended up with almost three times as many senators.

But the map with the new districts looked pretty funny. An artist saw the map of one county, Essex, where an absurdly shaped district ran around the edge. The artist could not resist sketching in head, wings, and claws, remarking, "That will do for a salamander!" And it did look very much like the lizardlike animal called the salamander. A newspaper editor who opposed Mr. Gerry was delighted. He immediately joined Gerry and salamander to form the word gerrymander.

The word caught on. People laughed and repeated the word gerrymander. Before long it was being used widely in the United States and Great Britain because it described something that people knew had been going on for a long time and they needed that word. And, being used so much in speaking and writing, gerrymander found its way into the dictionaries. It's still there.

Whether or not the word is just to Mr. Gerry, it is the only thing that remains of his name in history. He was one of the men who signed the Declaration of Independence. He attended the convention that drew up the Constitution in 1787. He was a member of Congress and was sent abroad to represent his country. He became Vice President of the United States. Yet you have to look him up in an encyclopedia to find out these things. Gerrymander is a word firmly established in the language to describe changing election district lines and thus taking an unfair advantage of your opponents in politics.

Shakespeare in his play *Julius Caesar* has the lines:

The evil that men do lives after them,
The good is oft interred with their bones.

But then, there is Pasteur.

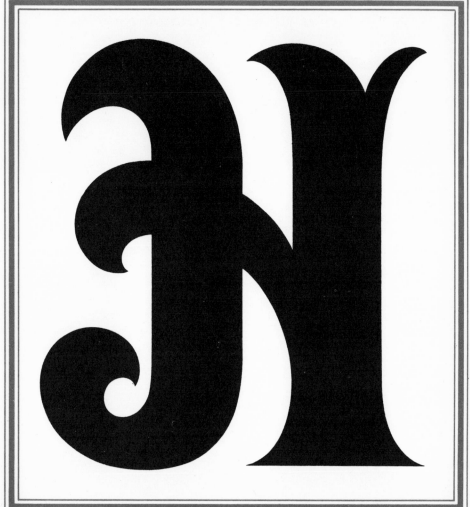

is for Heliotropism

H is for HELIOTROPISM

If you take a pot of flowers and put it near a window, you will find that as the sunlight grows strong in the morning the flowers turn their heads toward the window.

This is heliotropism. It is a word made up of the Greek word for sun, helios, and the Greek word for turning, trope. And there you have it. And you have also some idea of the power of light from the sun. The sun attracts, pulls things toward it. It can reach right down to earth and influence individual flowers. One flower that is especially influenced is called the heliotrope or turnsole, sol being the Latin word for sun. There are many varieties of this flower in many parts of the earth. The clusters are white to purple and very fragrant.

Insects may be strongly attracted to even a mild light, as you know from seeing moths and candleflies on a lighted window of a summer night. If they get into the house they are drawn irresistibly toward the lamps in the room. If there are candles they may fly into the open flame. This is an attraction akin to heliotropism and is known as phototropism, photo being from the Greek word for light.

The word heliotrope is more than three hundred years old in the English language, but heliotropism is not much more than one hundred years old. Heliotrope was the name given an ancient (you might say antediluvian) sundial, an instrument that showed the time of day by shadows as the sun turned or rose and set. Then men began to study plants. They discovered the plant most susceptible to the sun and named it heliotrope and they discovered the attraction the sun holds for many plants, and to describe this they made the word heliotropism.

Now we know that plants and insects are really not the only ones of God's creatures that are attracted by the sun. Men are too. There have been religions in the past based on the worship of the sun. And in our day we find people in the North following the sun to Florida or California in the winter. It is a fad to lie out in the sun and get tanned and show that you have been lying out in the sun. And sometimes people even put on a lotion or salve to make it look as if they had been lying out in the sun when they haven't.

Those most attracted to the sun in our day are scientists. They turn toward it the way plants do. They study it closely, especially when the moon passes between the sun and the earth and causes an eclipse. In 1868 there was a total eclipse of the sun visible in India and a scientist there guessed a gas on the sun that no one on earth had ever known before. Later another scientist investigated and confirmed the guess. A new element had been discovered on the sun before it was known on earth. Of course they named the new element helium. They even learned how to make it down here and then they found vast deposits of it under the earth's surface in the oilfields of Texas and Oklahoma. But the knowledge of it came first from the sun.

No wonder scientists are modern sun-worshipers. And no wonder they will go halfway around the earth to observe a total eclipse of the sun. There was one in 1937 that lasted longer than any eclipse had lasted in 1200 years — seven minutes and four seconds. It could best be studied from the waters of the Pacific Ocean. There were no great planes flying over water in those days, but the scientists got to the right spot with their instruments and were there and waiting when the moon's umbra fell across the face of the waters.

The more men work with the sun the more they respect its power. Their fascination is based on growing knowledge. And they know that the sun can harm as well as give life. Non-scientists may be attracted to the sun once in a while, say, during an eclipse. The may look at it through a smoked glass, not realizing that they can be blinded in this way. Men who know the sun have special equipment. They have an instrument that enables them to look at the sun without harming their eyes. You can guess what it's called. It's a helioscope, scope being from a Greek word meaning to look at. So they put the helioscope on the telescope and look at the sun in the distance and enjoy heliotropism as much as they please.

is for Innovation

I is for INNOVATION

When you hear of an innovation you know that somebody has introduced a new thing or a new way of doing things. The word comes from the Latin. The Latin word for new is novus, and when you see the shorter form nov in any word you can bet your bottom dollar that is will have to do with something new.

It is curious how almost everyone likes things that are new, often just because they are new. We get new shoes and keep calling them new and thinking of them as new for a long time, even when they begin to get scuffed. We respect what is new and treat it better than we do things that have been around for a long time.

That is the way it is with one of the words in our language. The word is novel. Your parents and teachers speak of a book that tells a made-up story as a novel. Well, a novel was once novel. It was an innovation, a new way of writing books. In the eighteenth century it was an innovation. There had long been long stories about imaginary people, but with the development of the printing press (after 1476 in England) this type of story became popular once more and in a slightly different form. The old became new again, so to say. To write a long story about people who didn't exist, to create characters and events, was at that time a novel thing to do. What was then new is now old, but we still call it novel.

An innovation, of course, can take many forms. You can find it in the way men and women dress. A quick change in styles that does not last is simply a fad or a craze, but if the change stays for a very long time, it is an innovation. Up until the time of President James Madison, who served from 1809 until 1817, the Presidents of the United States wore knee breeches and dressed the way statesmen in Europe did. But Mr. Madison decided to put on long trousers. This was a real innovation. You don't need to be told that it has lasted until our day.

If the President of the United States today came out in knee breeches and a wig, would it be an innovation? Well, it would certainly be a shock. No one can tell how long a style of dress will last. In Great Britain today the judges and bishops and certain high officials of state still wear wigs. There was a period of a hundred and fifty years, beginning around 1600, when men and women both wore wigs in Europe.

People like innovations. They like the new so much, in fact, that you hear people talking about "new innovations." This is saying enthusiastically more than is necessary. Innovation means something new has been introduced, and to speak of a new innovation is the same as speaking of a round circle. When we do this we are redundant. We are saying more than we ought to because we do not know the meaning of the word. A circle is round to begin with and an innovation is something new.

There are stores that sell what we call novelties, trinkets that are new or objects that once were new. One of these stores is called the five-and-ten, and the five-and-ten was a novelty, an innovation in fact, when it came on the American scene. There was nothing in it that cost more than twenty-five cents and you could get a big bag of candy for a nickel. Now the name five-and-ten hangs on like the name novel. Older folks keep calling a store that carries novelties the five-and-ten because that's the way they learned it.

One odd thing is that while we like things that are new we often don't like people who are new — and sometimes we don't like them simply because they are new. A person who is new on a job or tries to do something for the first time is called a novice. Novice is not a very favorable word, except in religious circles. When you say a fellow is a novice at a job it usually means that you think he doesn't know much. Another word with the novus root is novitiate. A novitiate is a learner, usually a religious learner, and people have respect for learners and even for those who plan to learn.

But it's the innovator we really like and admire. Thomas Jefferson had many unusual features built into his home, Monticello, near Charlottesville, Virginia. One was a bed that could be pulled up to the ceiling when it was not in use. It's still there and could be described in a way a young man described a clever antique not long ago: a two-hundred-year-old innovation.

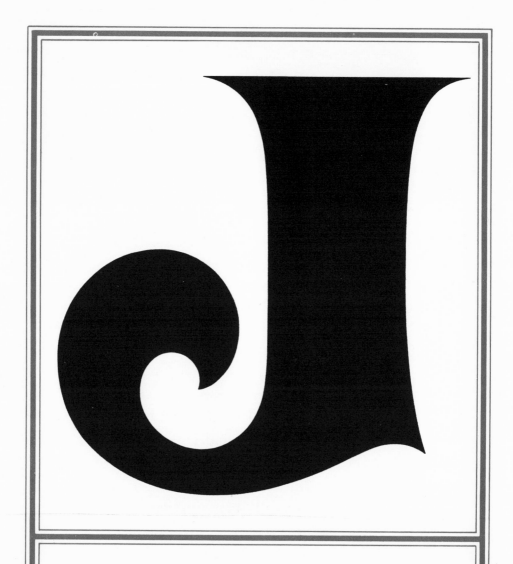

is for Journeyman

J is for JOURNEYMAN

The French language is by no means, not by a long shot, as big as the English language. One of our dictionaries has six hundred thousand entries in it. This means that we have a chance to use that many words. It gives us a wide range and we don't have to say a thing the same way twice.

French has only three hundred thousand words, but the French people know how to use words in such a way that they get the most mileage out of them. Their words are very expressive, and it is interesting that, with all the words we've got, we still borrow a great many from the French and call them our own. Menu, matinee, chic, naïve, and hors d'oeuvre are among them.

One of the French words we've borrowed and put to such wide use that it doesn't any longer look French is jour, the French word for day. Next time you eat out, ask your parents to show you the menu, and on it you'll probably find the term soup du jour. This means the soup that the restaurant is specializing in that particular day.

Think of the way jour shows up in other words that are familiar to you. Maybe you know someone who keeps a journal. He writes in it every day, or ought to. Or take the word journey. It was originally the distance one could go in a day. The day was the unit of measurement, as it was among the Indians in our country. When Indians started using English they would speak of the distance covered in a day as a sleep. There is a town in Wyoming now known as Ten Sleep. This meant that it was ten nights away from some spot. It marked the distance that could be traveled when one spent ten nights on the way.

A beautiful word built into our language from jour is the word journeyman. It has been with us a long time and has taken on various new meanings, all of them showing a form of respect and honor. A journeyman originally was one who worked for a day. He worked by the day, for a day's wages. This may not seem remarkable now, but it was rare then and it meant that he had finished his apprenticeship, no longer had to work for free but could be paid a day's wages.

The word thus came to mean that a man was a master of his craft. He was on his own and had proved his own skill, was not dependent on anything but his own hands and a chance to work. In our country the word told chiefly of journeymen printers, men who moved about the country, sometimes restlessly, always sure in a growing land of a job. You will meet one of these fellows as the Duke in *The Adventures of Huckleberry Finn*. When the Duke joins Huck and Jim on the raft he refers to himself as a "jour printer by trade." Jour or journeymen printers were men of words as a rule. The Duke could recite Shakespeare by the yard — not correctly, to be sure, but with love and eloquence.

Most journeymen printers loved the language, dealing as they did with type and the printed word. They enjoyed words and knew how to spell them, too, because they handled them every jour.

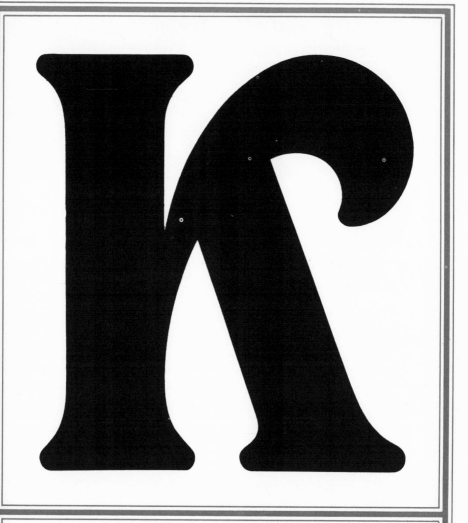

is for Knowledgeable

K is for KNOWLEDGEABLE

It doesn't sound reasonable, does it? K ought to stand for k'olegeable. You'd think that the n would be silent, as we say, and that the k would be sounded at the beginning of the word. Or that both ought to be pronounced because they are both there. In that case you would say kanowledgeable. And if you were speaking German, that is the way you would say the word. You would sound both the k and the n.

In small dictionaries, even, you will find a score or more of words that start with kn. These range from knack to knurl. And the point they have in common is that these words are German in origin and remain German in spelling as far as the first two letters are concerned. In German the word for boy is knabe, and the word is pronounced kanawba. In English we have the word knave, originally a serving lad. The English took a German word to describe a person of low status, but they changed the b to v and dropped the sound of the k to show that they had made the word their own. They made kanawba nave. But you can tell the

German parentage from the kn. Knowledgeable describes a person who knows a great deal, a person who has amassed a lot of information.

There is such delicate shading in words that a person can be said to be knowledgeable without really having knowledge. Knowledgeable is a complimentary word, something pleasant that people may say about you on the basis of the way you talk. But you alone know whether you have knowledge. It's the same way it is with reputation and character. Reputation tells what people think about you; character is what you are.

So being knowledgeable is not as important as having knowledge. Knowledge is a word of great dignity. It suggests wisdom. You do not really know a thing until you know it a long time and have had a chance to turn it over and over in your mind. Snap judgments about persons or ideas may now and then be right, but it is just as well to sleep over them, ruminate on them, and add to them from day to day both by picking up more information and by reflection.

Some words are deep and you never get to the bottom of them. Some words are showy and dazzling. Kaleidoscope is a delightful picture word. You can see colors the minute you see the word, colors dancing and whirling all over the room like miniature rockets. The word kaleidoscope was made up by Sir David Brewster, the man who invented the kaleidoscope in 1817. To form the word he took two Greek words, kalos, meaning beautiful, and eidos, meaning form, and, as you know, scope from a Greek word meaning to look at. The kaleidoscope breaks colors into beautiful forms for you to look at.

But once you've seen one kaleidoscope you've seen them all. Unless you are knowledgeable about color and study it, all those whirling spots, joyous though they are to the eye, remind you of bits and pieces of things you've learned but haven't put together into knowledge.

is for Lunarian

L is for LUNARIAN

Long before men had space ships they took flights of fancy, let their minds range among the planets, wandered and wondered about what was out there. More than two hundred and fifty years ago men thought there were people living on the moon. Neighbors in space. By 1708 these moon people seemed real enough to have a name. They were called lunarians, inhabitants of the moon.

The word was made from luna, the Latin word for moon. People who lived on the moon were lunarians, just as people who live in America are Americans. It was all pretty real because the moon itself has been so real and men have been very conscious of the moon and its closeness. It is close enough for you to see the face of the man in the moon when it is full. So it is no wonder that people on earth thought there were people on the moon.

Nowadays you don't hear the word lunarian used much, and if you do hear it, it means a student of the moon, one who observes the moon and thinks about its effects. These effects upon the earth are known and easy to see. The way great bodies of water are pulled about in sweeping motions that men call tides shows one effect. Sir Isaac Newton, who died in 1727, explained how the oceans were pulled by sun and moon and that the pull of the moon, since the moon is so close to the earth, is more than twice as great as that of the sun.

Men had thought long and hard about the effects of the moon. They thought the moon had a lot to do with the way people on earth behaved. They thought changes in the moon affected men's minds, and the word lunacy came into the language to describe a person whose behavior was awfully odd. A lunatic was a person thought to be crazy. And later the slang word loony came to describe in a kind of friendly and kidding way a person or conduct we think peculiar. Today we say, You're nuts.

The words lunacy, lunatic, and loony linger on to remind us of the old belief that there is some connection between human conduct and phases of the moon. Policemen tell us that we are likely to behave differently and more wildly on the night of the full moon than we do at other times. Whether it's an excuse built up by the word lunacy or the result of strange waves sent out by the moon or the lunarians living there, no one can prove. All we do know is that the full moon tends to make us loony and we have to watch ourselves when it appears.

Lunarian is a word that may come back into use as we go on with what men call the conquest of space. Meanwhile the word moon, which is German in origin, has taken over in popularity the place luna once had. And for a very simple reason. Moon is not a more beautiful word, but think how many more words it rhymes with. Can you thing of any word except tuna that rhymes with luna? What would the song writers do without the word moon? Lovers and men who write love songs are always aware of the big matchmaker in the sky and they like to call it the moon.

So moon is for romance and luna is for science. People sing about a harvest moon or the silvery moon, but astronomers speak of a lunar month — the time from one new moon to the next. We say that lovers under the spell of the moon are moonstruck, but we say that those who study the moon are lunarians. Those who sing speak of the moon; those who classify knowledge speak of luna. When scientists needed a name for the large North American moth with crescent-shaped spots on its wings, they named it, as you can guess, the luna moth.

That's the way it is with the family history of these two words — luna and moon.

is for Malapropism

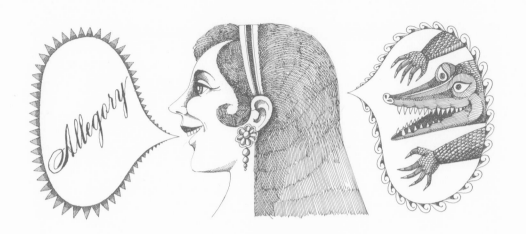

M is for MALAPROPISM

Whatever your gender, whether male or female, somebody could call you Mrs. Malaprop. A man can correctly be called Mrs. Malaprop. The woman never existed in real life, but she is famous just the same and you will find her listed in practically any dictionary you pick up, no matter how small. She has come to stand for a person who uses words carelessly, who makes mistakes of the ear and assumes that two words that sound alike are alike. It was many a Mrs. Malaprop who heard the word Forney as the name of a manufacturer of cheap jewelry and turned it into phony. No harm done, to be sure, and there is no harm done as a rule with malapropisms. They just show what an inattentive ear most of us have.

Mrs. Malaprop is a character in *The Rivals,* a play by the distinguished English dramatist Richard Sheridan. It was produced first in 1775 and became one of the most popular plays of the English theater. Sheridan took the French term mal à propos, chopped off the last two letters and made a proper name of it.

Anyone who knew enough to go to the theater knew that mal à propos meant not appropriate.

Sheridan gave Mrs. Malaprop appropriate lines, lines in which she mixed words that sounded alike. She would speak of an allegory on the banks of the Nile — instead of an alligator. And she would say affluence when she meant influence.

Is it any wonder that Mrs. Malaprop became popular and stayed that way? She reminded people of people who make this kind of mistake all the time, including themselves. There was the little boy who said, "I must go to Sunday school today because I'm going to get a reward." What he was going to get was an award. George Eliot spoke of what she called a malapropian friend who said she was sending a missile instead of a missive. Mistakes that lead to malapropisms happen through the ear. One man with a new secretary dictated a lot of letters and ended them with Very truly yours. When they came back for signature, they read Virtually yours.

It is curious how the language needs words now and then and they are suddenly supplied — in many cases by the stage, where people can hear them used and let them nestle in their ears comfortably because they know how they are pronounced. Take the word robot. It belongs to our age. It is one of the newest words in the language and one of the quickest to be accepted and it came from the stage. In 1922 there was a play on Broadway in New York called *R.U.R.* (Rossum's Universal Robots). The word robot came from the Czech word meaning drudge, a tedious worker, a worker so bored by what he did that he hardly knew he was doing it. In the play a robot was a human who acted automatically. By 1925 the word was in the dictionary to describe a machine that worked without thinking.

The world was ready for the word robot, just as it was ready in 1775 and later for Mrs. Malaprop. And malapropism will always be good.

Listen hard for the next few days and see how many times people say what they don't mean and don't know it.

If you do this, it will help you cultivate an accurate and sensitive ear for words. But don't let the fear of malapropisms of your own keep you from using words you hear and like. It's good to use words out loud and listen to them in or with your own ear. That is the way you get used to them and learn to love their melodies. If you're wrong in the way you first use a new word, somebody will be sure to tell you. You may be slightly embarrassed, but no one was ever hanged for a malapropism.

is for Mnemonics

MN is for MNEMONICS

This is a good word to remember because it is a word that tells you about the art or science of remembering. And if you can remember how to spell it, you can remember anything. It comes from a Greek word that means reminding and remembering. When you say mnemonics out loud, the m is silent. You just forget it when you say the word, but you remember the m when you spell it. Remember the s at the end, too. Mnemonics is what is known as a plural noun. It sounds as if there were more than one, but you say mnemonics is, not mnemonics are — just as you would say politics is, not politics are.

There is so much to remember about it that mnemonics is a kind of memory lesson all in one word. It's been around in English since the early days of the eighteenth century, which shows you how long people have been trying to work out ways of reminding themselves to remember. There are men who seriously study the problem of memory and make up systems and even sell them. And of course everybody has some sort of system or method. One of the simplest is the trick of tying a string around the finger. The practice of using string for a reminder is at least a thousand years old. In Peru the Incas took knotted cords called quipus and made them into an elaborate system of remembering even tax records and stories. Thus there is good precedent for tying a string around your finger. Everybody knows it helps — if you can remember why the string is there.

Whether it works or not, tying a string around the finger and using it as an aid to memory is a sample of mnemonics. There are lots of others. One is to think backwards when you have lost something — retrace your steps in your mind. There was once a cartoon which showed an elegant and wealthy lady saying to her ne'er-do-well son, "Now think back, Reginald. Where did you leave your yacht?"

How do you remember names? You will find that all people are proud of their names, sensitive about them, and pleased if you remember them. So you'll certainly need mnemonics practically every day. One scheme is to associate a person's name with something you already know. You meet a Mr. Richards. You say rich instantly and try to remember his name that way. You can usually find something in every name that you can tie around your finger.

One of the interesting problems of life is to remember the future — what you are supposed to do tomorrow. And one of the best ways of doing it is to make lists or notes to yourself. Or if you are to take something with you when you go out, put it at the door where you can't miss it.

Any change in routine helps jog the memory, as the saying goes. If your mother's car is low on gas, she may take the keys out and put them in a different place. This will remind her. Only she'd better remember where she put them.

Mnemonics is important because it helps to keep the mind in charge of what we do. There are many reasons why we forget. One reason may be that we don't want to do what we are supposed to do and we put it out of our minds. You say you forgot — and you did. But you know, deep down, that you are fooling yourself. Mnemonics will help you be honest with yourself and know your feelings better.

The word reminds us of all those people who have been trying so long to think up ways of remembering. You can study what they have done and take advantage of how much they have learned. Maybe before you're through your mnemonics will be the best yet.

is for Nostalgia

N is for NOSTALGIA

You may know a book called *The Incredible Journey*. It was written by Sheila Burnford, and the three animals in it are brought beautifully to life by the writer and through the pictures drawn by the artist Carl Burger. It is a hard-to-believe and gripping story of an old bull terrier named Bodger, a young Labrador retriever named Luath, and of a Siamese cat, Tao. As the story opens, these animals are staying in the home of a friend of the family who owns them. Their owners have gone on a long trip to England. The animals are well cared for and seem to be contented, but the young retriever gets a deep longing in his bones to go home. He leads the others and they set out across almost three hundred miles of Canadian wilderness to find their real home.

What Bodger, Luath and Tao had was a bad case of nostalgia. Nostalgia is not always as bad as it was in the case of *The Incredible Journey*, but often it is. A loneliness for familiar home surroundings, for the sights and sounds and tastes and smells of things we like to have around us, is a feeling that is very deep in men and women and boys and girls as well as in animals. We miss what we love, what is our very own, even if it's only an old shoe or a familiar bed. We miss the familiar and there are times when we are sick to get back to it.

No wonder, then, that there is a very old word to describe the sickness all of us have felt. Nostalgia is the classic word for this feeling. It is made up from two Greek words — nostos, for a return home, and algos, for pain. In English algos becomes algia, and when you see algia as a suffix you know that the word has something to do with pain. In neuralgia, for example, it is tacked to the Greek word for nerves, neura, and tells of the acute pain that comes from an inflammation of the nerves.

So originally nostalgia was thought of as such a painful form of melancholy that it had the kind of pain that comes with a disease. And when the Anglo-Saxon synonym came into the language later, you will notice that it was homesickness, not home-longing or homewishing. People showed by both the words, nostalgia and homesickness, that they often experienced a kind of illness when they wanted to return to their home or home town or homeland.

Of course words get quieter and kinder as they get older, and while there are still cases of homesickness and there always will be, the word nostalgia has come to mean a kind of pleasant long-ing, a mood, a thing that flits through the mind and makes us remember or re-remember. When we remember again and again, we reminisce. That is what reminiscence means, and it is related in a way to nostalgia.

It's got to a point now where we rather enjoy nostalgia. We like to read and hear about the nostalgia of others, be they dogs and cats or men. You may have seen grown-ups reach for the paper handkerchiefs when they hear a beautiful voice singing "Home, Sweet Home." They may be in their own homes when they hear it on the radio or on a record, yet they find it deeply moving. They are remembering a time when they were not home and longed to be. They've got a mild attack of nostalgia and don't mind it much.

is for Onomatopoeia

O is for ONOMATOPOEIA

Take the word buzz. Anyone who has heard a bumblebee flying around knows that the word buzz sounds like the noise the bee makes. Well, buzz is an example of onomatopoeia.

Onoma is the Greek word for name, and onomatopoeia comes from this word and another Greek word which means to make. The word onomatopoeia really tells you about words that are made from sounds. The word repeats the sound. Kerchoo sounds the way persons do when they sneeze. What does soda water do but fizz? Clang is the noise a bell makes and it is the word for the noise a bell makes. A bullet strikes a surface sharply and it pings. Ping-pong is the name of a game that comes from the sounds the hollow ball makes on the table and on the paddle.

Chickadee and whippoorwill are names given to birds because the words make the same sound that the birds make. Bobwhite is also a name given a bird (the American quail) after its call. It is great sport to play echo with a bobwhite. When he gives his call, you whistle back: bobwhite. You call back and forth this way for a while. He may later repeat his first name and call bob-bobwhite. You echo this call and then later you say bob-bobwhite, and if he answers in the same way, you've got an unseen friend.

The many, many onomatopoeias you will find listed in the dictionaries are marked echoic. They say the same thing that the sound says. Echo was a lovely maiden in Greek legend who was a brilliant talker, but she incurred the wrath of the goddess Hera and was condemned to wander all over the earth and say nothing — only to repeat what had been said. To make matters worse she fell in love with Narcissus, was rejected, wasted away until nothing was left of her but her voice. Now and then you can talk to her if you get the right range of hills, but you can also find her in words that give back the sounds that we give to them.

When trains made nice noises and steam engines panted and talked like *The Little Engine That Could* (I think I can, I think I can, I think I can), boys imitated the sounds of trains, including their long and mournful whistles. Now they can imitate the sounds of fire engines and sirens, sometimes scaring their mothers from the back seat. These are samples of onomatopoeia, expressing the wish we all have to form these noises we hear into words.

You will find instances of onomatopoetic language in poetry. One of the best examples is "The Bells" by Edgar Allan Poe. In this beautiful poem Poe uses words and flowing lines to give the sound of all manner of bells. He speaks of bells keeping time, time, time —

To the tintinnabulation that so musically wells
From the bells, bells, bells, bells,
Bells, bells, bells
From the jingling and the tinkling of the bells.

Tintinnabulation comes from the Latin word tintinnabulum, a little bell, which comes from another Latin word, tintinnare, to jingle. So in tintinnabulation we have a Latin onomatopoeia carried over into English and sounding as if we made it up ourselves.

Before long you may get the impression that practically all words are onomatopoeia. You might suspect ooze and bubble, but they are not — not in origin. Slam is, though. It's from the Norwegian, slamra. They thought of it first.

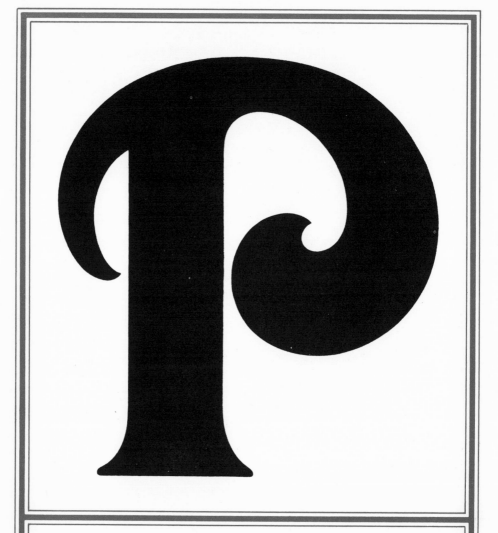

is for Pusillanimous

P is for PUSILLANIMOUS

Pusillanimous is a name-calling word. It is an adjective, and an adjective is a word that tells you something a little extra about a person or thing. You may say that a man has a hat or you may say that he has a green hat. Green is the adjective.

There are some mortals who take pleasure from insulting their fellows. They are fond of adjectives, of using words to describe the way they think other people are. Pusillanimous is a word that such people can use to their hearts' content. If you are one of them, you can either tell a fellow that he's chicken-hearted or you can tell him he's pusillanimous. It's a hard choice. If you say he's chicken-hearted, he will know what you mean — and the chances are he won't know what you mean if you accuse him of being pusillanimous. He might even think it's something worse than it is.

And it's not really a bad word. It's just not a pleasing word. It comes from two Latin words, pusillus, which means very small, and animus, the word for mind or spirit. So a person who is said

[73]

to be pusillanimous is thought of as having a very small mind or a very weak spirit.

Gradually pusillanimous has come to describe a weak spirit rather than a small mind. Back in 1611 a man wrote that "there are tears of manliness as well as tears that are womanish and pusillanimous." Being womanish and being pusillanimous were made to seem one and the same thing — at least in the man's view. If a thing wasn't manly, it was weak. So men started using the word pusillanimous to mean that another man lacked courage.

That's the way you will find it used nowadays. The synonym of pusillanimous is cowardly. Synonym comes from two Greek words and means to have the same name. The antonym (or opposite) of pusillanimous is brave.

One good thing about pusillanimous, in spite of its meaning, is that it's a fat and comical word and hard to take seriously. It is rolypoly and musical and it cannot hurt like a small word that jabs. It's the kind of word you would use in a pillow-fight with words. Besides, there are some traits of character worse than those pusillanimous describes. You can be a very acceptable person — even with no great brain and no great bravery. After all, there was Winnie-the-Pooh.

more
to
come

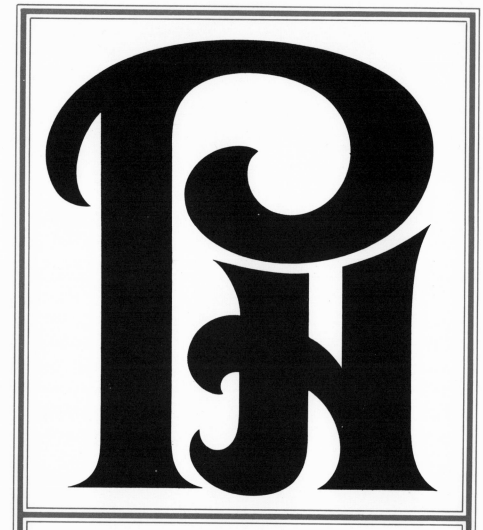

is for Philanthropy

PH is for PHILANTHROPY

Many words have many meanings or shades of meaning and they mean one thing one time and something else another. But some words just come right out and say what they mean.

This is true of philanthropy. It means the love of man, the love men have for the race as a whole. That is what it means in origin, in the way it is put together, and that is what it means in fact. And it's rather marvelous that the word has not been corrupted. That's probably because it had so much character and beauty to begin with.

In Greek phil means loving and anthropos designates man. The word philanthropy has been in English use since 1608. With all of man's inhumanity to man that has been recorded since that date, still the fact and the word of philanthropy remain to remind us that there is much of good in the race. What is more, philanthropy is a word always tied up with action. It is tied up with giving. Most people who hear of our philanthropists and philanthropic enterprises have come to think that philanthropy means giving away money. That is the way the word has got itself known, probably because so many people have so little money that they think it's the most important thing on earth. So they speak of a man who gives away great sums of money as a philanthropist. Henry David Thoreau said that philanthropy is the only virtue that is sufficiently appreciated by mankind.

You don't have to be rich to be generous or to show your love of humankind. If you take the real meaning of the word philanthropy, you can see that there are many things to give besides money. Ideas, for example. We might say that Mohandas K. Gandhi, the great Hindu leader who was assassinated in 1948, was as much of a philanthropist as Andrew Carnegie, who gave away millions of dollars to found libraries in small towns. Or would you say that Gandhi was an even greater philanthropist? He was penniless, but he gave the modern world the principle and the example of nonviolence.

Both phil and philo are nice words from the Greek to remember because they turn up in many words and they always mean something that has to do with love. When you know that biblio means book, you can tell that the strange word philobiblic describes a man who is fond of books. Sometimes phil turns up at the end of a word, as in bibliophile, meaning also a man who loves books. Philo combined with sophos, which is the Greek word for wise, to form philosopher, one who loves wisdom, or at least loves being wise. And you can see at a glance or hear out of one ear that philharmonic means a love of harmony.

Keep an eye and ear open for phil and philo in the puzzle of big words. They will always show a friendly face and help you find the central meaning, as in Philadelphia, the city of Brotherly Love. And it is amusing to note that even the name Philip, made popular by five Kings of Macedon way before the time of Christ, comes from the Greek word philippos, meaning fond of horses. Even great warriors who swung the sword loved something, if only their horses.

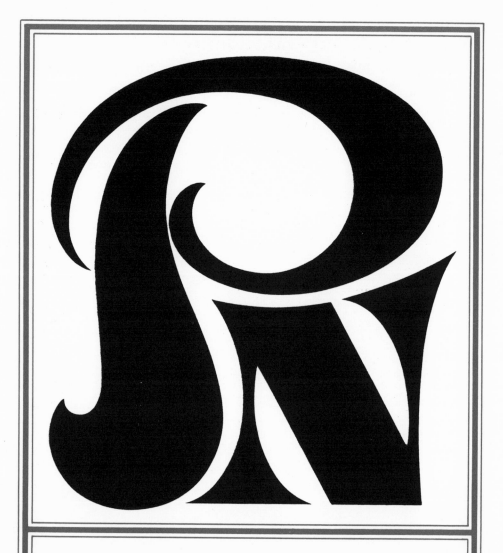

is for Pneumatotherapy

PN is for PNEUMATOTHERAPY

Pneuma is a word of great dignity, a very old word, to describe what is probably the most important thing to all of us. Pneuma is the Greek word for breath, for the breath of life. It deals with the great mystery of life. In the Christian religion the Pneuma is a name for the Holy Spirit.

In our everyday speech we put pneuma to some pretty lowly or commonplace uses. For example, we speak of a pneumatic tire, meaning one that has air in it, not one that is solid. You ride around all the time on pneumatic tires, and if you wanted to be very literal in your talk you could say that you ride around on the breath of life.

Pneumatotherapy is the practice of treating disease by the use of rarefied or condensed air. It is a new practice and a fairly new word made up out of old ones, for therapy is a word that also comes from the Greek. In Greek therapeia means care or treatment, and when you see the word therapy by itself or in other words you know that it means someone is trying to care for or treat someone.

You will find pneuma in other words as well. Pneumonia, once a disease that took the lives of many persons before the days of modern miracle drugs, is a disease of the lungs, of the breathing apparatus. That terrible noise workmen make when they are tearing up a pavement is made with a pneumatic drill, one that uses compressed air.

When you get into zoology and begin to study various kinds of animals, you will find that some are pneumonophorous. You will know from pneu that these must be animals that use air to live on. Some don't. Some are non-pneumonophorous. It's a good way to classify animals and to find that there is more to facts than meets the eye. You would say that lions have lungs and live on land and they are pneumonophorous. And that fish are not. Yet there is the lungfish, which has both gills and lungs and can live on air or water as it chooses. It's a very convenient state and would save a lot of drownings if we were all that way, wouldn't it? And the biggest fishlike animal of all, the whale, is pneumonophorous. Whales live in the sea and yet breathe air. Seals and otters are pneumonophorous. They can live on both sea and land. They are what you call amphibious, which means that they lead a double life. Amphibious is made up of the Greek word amphi, meaning on both sides, and bios, meaning life. Remember — you find bios in many other words, including biography, the written story of a man's life.

No matter how big the word, you can find some clue in it. In pneumatotherapy it is there in pneuma. Whenever you see pneu or pneuma, you know that the word has something to do with air and breath and lungs. One writer says that gannets, birds that resemble pelicans, swim lightly although they are heavy. This, he explains, is owing to the pneumaticity of their bodies.

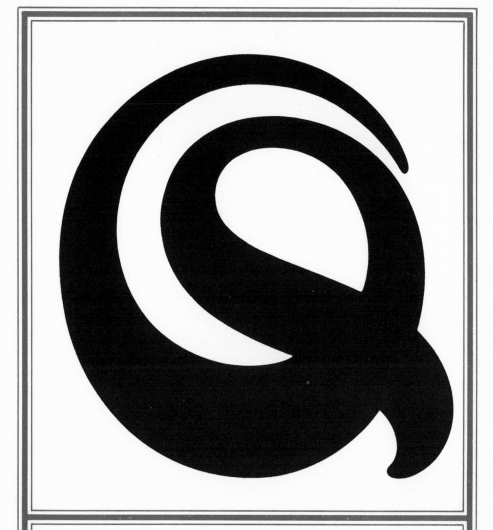

is for Quintessence

Q is for QUINTESSENCE

If you love a mystery, quintessence is your word. It will take you the rest of your life to find out what it actually means, yet the odd part of it is that you know already. Ralph Waldo Emerson speaks of the Greek gods sitting around and discussing quintessence and sunbeams. That's pretty high talk, isn't it? You really don't know what a sunbeam is, and yet you know it is there. Sometimes a sunbeam looks strong enough to swing from and that is why it is called a beam. But you can't hang on it and it is very hard to tell what a sunbeam is.

It is hard to tell what quintessence is, too, but the way the word came into being and what it meant to those who made it up will help toward understanding it.

Most men of olden times believed that there were four things or elements all around us all the time. Only four. They were named air, fire, water, and earth. These were things you could see or feel or smell. But wise men knew also that there must be something else, some mystery they could not describe but must stand in awe of. Men who thought believed that the heavenly bodies were made up of something besides the four main things that we know about. These heavenly bodies must be made up of an extra something or essence and to this extra essence they gave the name quintessence.

It was natural to give such a name when men thought a lot in Latin, for quint is a carryover into English of the Latin word for fifth: quinta. So quintessence means literally the fifth essence beyond the four that we deal with every day. You will find quint in other words, and you can guess that the word in which you find quint has to do with fifth or five. You hear occasionally that five babies have been born to the same mother, and you know that they are called quintuplets. If you are playing word games with a friend and he says he'll double something and you triple it and he quadruples it, you get ahead when you quintuple it. You hear of a basketball team of five men called a quintet or see it referred to in newspaper headlines as a quint.

These words may seem a far cry from quintessence, but they help you think of quint as the fifth essence — the essence you can't see but can feel in your bones. Alchemists of the Middle Ages were so sure that quintessence was real, and merely hidden in all things, that they thought they could find it and make it as real as air or water. Others were content to give the mysterious substance a name and wag their heads.

People like to remind themselves of mysteries by giving mysterious names. It's a good practice. And it's the real value of the word quintessence. It shows us that, no matter how much we know, there is always something we don't understand, and that we ought to remind ourselves of this fact with a word. It is a beautiful word because there is a beautiful idea back of it. Men who use it are searching for a way to say what they can't see but know is real just the same. Hamlet speaks of man as "the quintessence of dust."

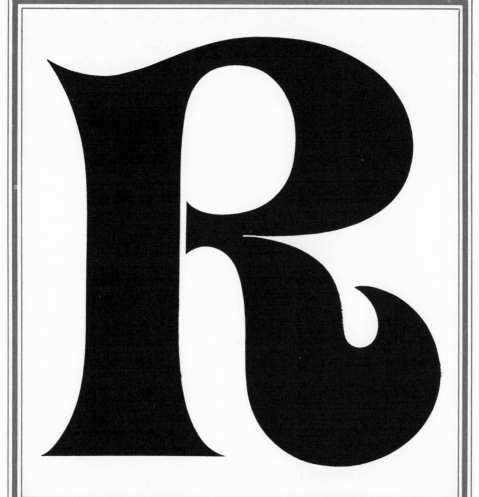

is for Ruminate

R is for RUMINATE

If you could ruminate you could swallow your food whole, not just half-whole the way you do when you are in a hurry. It would go into the first of four stomachs, known as the rumen and looking like bubble gum. Then you could bring your food back up when you got good and ready and chew it.

That is the way cattle, buffalo, sheep, antelope, camels, giraffes, llamas and other animals (known as ruminants) work out the food problem. They are busy gobbling grass or hay for a while and then they lie down later and enjoy their meal in the form of a cud, this being from an Anglo-Saxon word, cwudu, meaning like a ball. It's fun to watch them. They look so leisurely and content when they are chewing their cuds.

It's hardly feasible, of course, for humans or horses to do this, because humans and horses have only one stomach. Yet you will hear people say they are going to ruminate, or that they want to ruminate over something. They have been saying this, off and on, for more than four hundred years. You can see what an impression on people animals make when they chew their cuds. When people speak of themselves as ruminating they mean they are going to think over something later and not decide at the moment. They are going to sleep over it, yes. But more, they are going to take it in fast and bring it up again and think about it actively when they have the time. One of Shakespeare's characters spoke of wanting "to ruminate my grief." He would relive it. And the poet Pope has a character who is "ruminating wrath." He had to get mad all over again.

When we take a word like ruminate and use it the way we do we are making what we call a figurative use of the word. When animals were a part of every person's daily life and could be seen in the manger or the field, everyone knew about cud-chewing. So when a person said he wanted to ruminate you knew that he meant to use the picture of the animal to show what was going on in his mind.

The mind likes to work in pictures that are familiar to it. A pilot of a giant jet that plies the skies across the Atlantic may speak of pouring on coal when he opens the throttles for full take-off speed. We know one who does. In his boyhood, locomotives burned coal, and when the engineer wanted to get up full steam (get his boiler full of steam), the fireman shoveled on coal as fast as he could. You could see the black smoke pouring out of the smokestack and you knew that the engine would soon go much faster.

Well, that's a long way from chewing your cud. But that's the way it is with words. One picture leads to another. Just read it now and ruminate later.

more
to
come

is for Sesquipedalian

S is for SESQUIPEDALIAN

You know from pedal in sesquipedalian that this word has something to do with foot. You might as well know the rest right away and figure it out later. Sesquipedalian, for all its length and pleasant noises, simply means foot-and-a-half.

Sesqui, the first part of sesquipedalian, is a contraction. That is to say, it is made up of two Latin words run together. We run words together in our language all the time. We say can't instead of can not and don't instead of do not. Sesqui is made up of the Latin term semis, which means half, and que, which means and or in addition. Put them together in sesqui and you have a term that means more by a half.

You won't find sesqui in many words until you get into chemistry, but it is a very useful part of one word you will see now and then — sesquicentennial. When a town or country or perhaps a business celebrates its hundredth anniversary, it has its centennial. But we like to celebrate anniversaries and we don't like to wait a hundred years every time. So now and then there is a celebration of a hundred-and-fiftieth anniversary. When we do this we have a sesquicentennial. Whatever is celebrated is more than a hundred years old by a half. How else could you say it?

Sesquipedalian is a clown word, and it is not used in any but a light or comic sense. For more than 1900 years it has been a term of exaggeration to show how big or tall something is. Horace, who died in 8 B.C., spoke of sesquipedalian words. Sesquipedalian itself is one of them. It seems and sounds as if it were a foot-and-a-half long. In our day we speak of big words or long words we don't know as two-dollar words or as jawbreakers. One writer calls them dachshund words. But sesquipedalian is still around when you want to describe something in an amused way as much longer or bigger than it actually is; you can safely say that it is sesquipedalian.

There is probably another reason why sesquipedalian has stayed long and comfortably in the language. It is not only comical; it is also musical. Write it like a poem and you will hear all the appealing sounds in it:

> *Ses*
> > *qui*
> > > *pe*
> > > > *da*
> > > > > *li*
> > > > > > *an*

It has a nice accent and it scans. The emphasis falls in such a way that you seem to be reciting a poem when you roll it around and off your tongue. It seems to go on and on in your mind after you have finished saying it.

The British occasionally smile at us because we Americans use big words for very simple things — words of Latin origin instead of those from Anglo-Saxon roots. For example, we say elevator and they say lift. One British writer notes that "a certain sesqui-pedalianism is natural to Americans." Well, we're a big country and like things that are big.

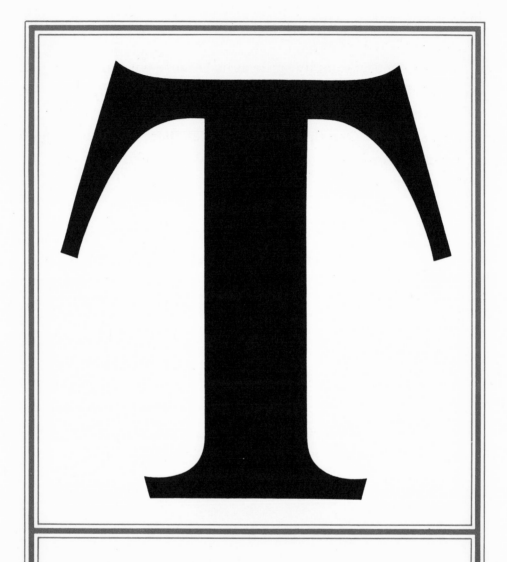

is for Transcendentalism

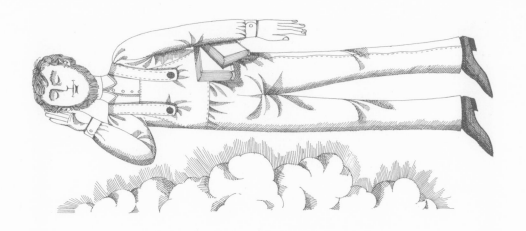

T is for TRANSCENDENTALISM

Transcendentalism is probably the longest nickname in the English language. It is a nickname given the beliefs of a group of people who began writing and thinking in New England during the 1840's. Some people thought the Transcendentalists were a little group of serious thinkers and others thought they were a serious group of little thinkers. Almost all agreed that the Transcendentalists were odd. They believed, these Transcendentalists, in quintessence, that there was more to the world than meets the eye.

As you know, a nickname can poke fun at people. Or it can be used affectionately. Sometimes it can be used both ways. Transcendentalism was a kind of pet name for thinkers—among them Ralph Waldo Emerson and Henry David Thoreau—whose views were above the views of other thinkers of their day. To get some idea of how different those views seemed, let's take the word transcendentalism apart and put it together again.

The prefix trans comes from an old Latin verb meaning to pass, and when you see it in our language, as you often will, it means beyond or across. In transportation the prefix trans joins with another Latin verb, portare, to carry. When you transport something, you carry it across or beyond. If a train or plane goes all the way across the country, it is a transcontinental train or plane.

In transcendentalism the prefix trans joins a form of the Latin verb, scandere, meaning to climb. You find other forms of this verb in such words as ascend and descend — to climb up and to climb down. When writers were called Transcendentalists, then, it meant that they had climbed with or in their minds to get up where they could see things better. They were up there looking down and seeing the world from a new point of view. You have done this yourself. You take flights of fancy and the world doesn't look the same as it does when you are earthbound. There is a little bit of transcendentalism in all of us, and don't let anybody tell you anything different, either.

You are in good company with the Transcendentalists. They rose above the dead level of dull daily talk. They believed in the power of the mind, that the mind was mightier than the sword and that great things could be accomplished through thought. They brought new ideas to America, ideas that came in part from European and Oriental philosophers and in part from the habit the Transcendentalists had of thinking beyond what you can see all around you.

It's a big word you won't see every day or even once a week, but you'll see it off and on all your life. And it will mean more and more to you as time goes on.

more
to
come

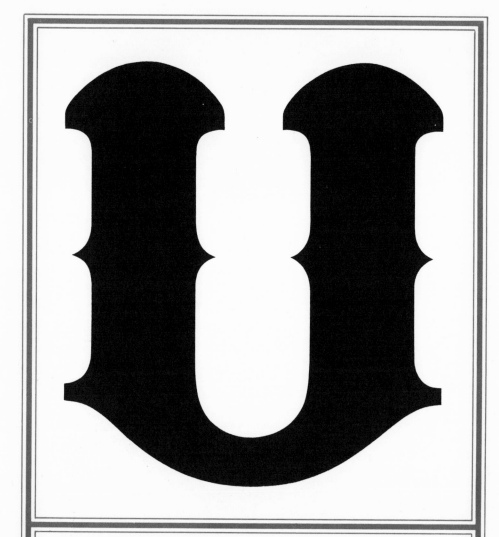

is for Umbrageous

U is for UMBRAGEOUS

Umbrageous is a funny word. It looks funny, like a shaggy dog on paper, and it sounds funny, as if someone were making it up as he said it. Yet it is a serious word also — sad and rather pathetic, in fact, because it has lost its character. Words can be ruined by people, just as children can get a bad name by associating with companions who put them up to mischief.

Somewhere along the way umbrageous got into bad company. It used to mean shady, and now it means touchy, irascible, easy to anger, suspicious. At least this is the way you hear it used nowadays if you hear it used at all. Yet the poet Percy Bysshe Shelley, who lived from 1792 to 1822, spoke of "the umbrageous loveliness of the surrounding country." And Alexander Pope, another English poet, who was born in 1688 and died in 1744, speaks of umbrageous leaves in a grove of trees.

Not long ago a mother wrote of her young son, "He looked umbrageous when I told him he couldn't go to kindergarten because of his cold."

What changed the meaning of the word so that it could be used to describe a person who looks offended? People began to use it to mean dark rather than shady. It comes from the Latin word umbra, meaning shade or shadow. When shadows get deep they become dark, and almost everyone is a little suspicious of the dark. Villains, you know, have dark hair and complexion and often a black mustache. They ride black horses. Could it be that as long ago as 1601, when people started using umbrageous to mean suspicious, it was already a habit to see everything in terms of black and white?

Sooner or later you will hear someone say, possibly to you, "Well, don't take umbrage." This simply means, although the person who says it may not know it, that a shadow has fallen across your face. Something inside of you has made you look gloomy. Your countenance darkens, as the old writers used to put it.

Taking umbrage is what is known as an idiom. Idiom comes from the Greek word idioma and means a peculiar use of words. In an idiom words are put together in a way that gives a meaning to them that they don't have separately. Taking umbrage is not the same as taking medicine. Come to think of it, however, when you take medicine, if it tastes bad, you will probably take umbrage at the same time — because your countenance will darken. Robert Louis Stevenson has one of his characters ask his host, "May I help myself to wine without umbraging you?"

You can find umbra in other words. You find it in umbrella, a canopy raised on a stick to give shade. Whenever you find umbra or even part of it in a word you can be sure that the word has something to do with shade. One useful word is adumbrate. It means, among other things, to sketch or outline in a shadowy way. It means also and literally to foreshadow, being made up quite simply of the Latin prefix ad, meaning action or movement toward, plus umbra. When you walk along with the sun behind your back, the shadow ahead of you adumbrates your coming. It shows that there is something to come besides what you see. That something is you. So adumbrate can mean to foretell from the shade or shadow you see.

A word you can enjoy all your life is penumbra. This word is made up of the Latin paene, meaning almost, and our old friend umbra. A penumbra is a light shadow seen along with a darker one. When the moon is in full eclipse, for example, you will see a light area or lesser shadow around the rim of it, and that will be a penumbra. But you don't have to wait for an eclipse of the moon. Every day or even at night when there are two or three lights in a room, you will see a penumbra. When you see two shadows, one dark and the other light, the light one is a penumbra.

Now go sit in the umbrage and think it over.

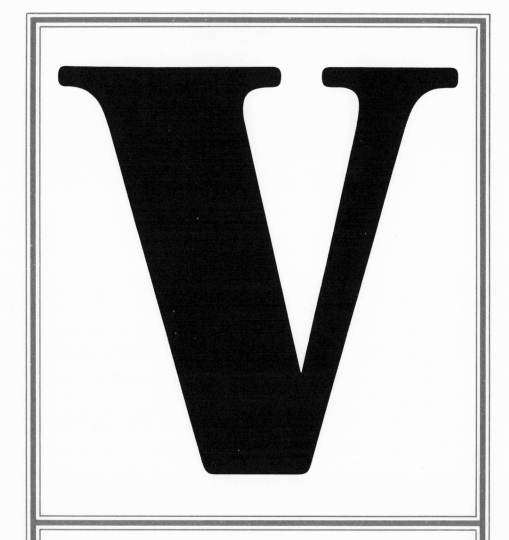

is for Valedictorian

V is for VALEDICTORIAN

Maybe you know some boy or girl in your town who will be valedictorian this year. A valedictorian is a person who makes the best grades and as a sort of reward or honor gets a chance to stand up at the end of the school year, at graduation time, and say goodbye in behalf of the class. That is what a valedictorian does. He or she delivers a valedictory, which is a farewell address.

Farewell means exactly what it says. You take leave of people and want them to fare well while you are away. That is the meaning of vale in valedictory. Vale is a form of the Latin verb valere, which expresses the hope that people will keep strong and in good health. Val is one of those spot syllables you will find repeated in many words, and it always has to do with health or strength. You may hear people say that an excuse is valid, which means that it is good and healthy. Or an object has value — it's good and strong. Or a man is valiant — he's good and strong.

You can find vale in a wonderful word, valetudinarian. A valetudinarian is a person in poor health or one who thinks he is. He is always very, very careful about his health. He thinks about it and studies ways to look out for his health. Sometimes he worries about his health so much that he makes himself sick. But right at the beginning is vale, and the interesting point is that a valetudinarian *wants* to be strong.

Valedictorian is made up of vale and another Latin term — dicere, meaning to speak. You can trace forms of dicere in a lot of other words and get to a point where you recognize it. People will tell you to watch your diction, your manner of speaking. Dictionaries tell us about speech and the way words are used. A Dictaphone is something you speak into and hear speech come back from. A dictum is a saying, usually authoritative.

There are many ways of speaking and all of them tell you something about people. The Russians have a wonderful word that begins with v. It is vranyo. The word and the way it is used tells you that the Russians are great kidders. They like to tell tales to each other and to visitors, tales they don't want to have taken seriously, that you are not supposed to take literally and at the same time you are not to deny. There is a game in the word vranyo. A Russian may tell a visitor that he can go into Moscow's Lenin Library and find English and American books that criticize the Russian system. The visitor is to play like he believes the story or at least doesn't disbelieve it. He shows that he does not understand vranyo if he insists that the Russian take him to the library and prove what was said.

There is a lot of vranyo in all of us. You have heard children say that they are going to run away. They mean it and yet they don't. And grown-ups are supposed to play the game and half-believe. Or your father may say that he is going to quit his job if the boss doesn't do so-and-so. It's an American form of vranyo.

It's a good word to keep in mind to keep out of arguments with. Don't take everything you hear too seriously. And it won't hurt to practice a little vranyo yourself. Tell yourself you are going to grow up and be a valedictorian. No one will quite believe you for a while, and then you can grow up and be one and fool everybody twice.

is for Wanderlust

W is for WANDERLUST

The bear went over the mountain, the old song tells us, to see what he could see. He had wanderlust. He had no high and mighty purpose. He was simply curious and had an itching foot. He liked to wander and take a look at whatever caught his fancy. It might be bright red berries that were good to munch. It might be an old stump that looked for a second like another bear standing on its hind legs. It might be the view from the top of the mountain, so that he could look off into the blue distance and watch the layers of colors that got deeper and deeper the farther away they were and he could let his mind wander as he stood there blinking, not thinking or thinking about thinking, but blinking, just blinking, and loving the vastness of all that was about him.

Wanderlust is not confined to bears, as every boy knows. It's just that bears have more time for it and more opportunity. And it takes time to wander. Of course, if you haven't got time or opportunity, you can sometimes make both. There used to be a comic strip (about the time your grandparents were the age you are now) that told of the doings of a boy named Jimmie. His mother would send him out, say, to get meat for dinner. But he always found as he went something that interested him and he would turn aside to explore it. In all the years that the strip ran Jimmie never really ran an errand. It was hard on his mother, but he had fun and so did all those who followed his gaddings and felt the way he did.

There is a very old Persian fairy tale called "The Three Princes of Serendip." They were not unlike Jimmie. They were forever discovering things they were not looking for and finding that these things that they turned aside to see were more important than what they had set out to find. Serendip was the ancient name for Ceylon, so the practice of wandering is a very old one in our literature. In 1754 an English writer, Horace Walpole, made up the word serendipity, based on the story of "The Three Princes of Serendip," to describe the luck people often have in finding the best things accidentally.

The word wanderlust itself comes from two very old words. Both are German. Wander is akin to wend. You will hear it said that a river wends its way through the fields. Torrents rush and so do some rivers. But others move slowly, first in one direction and then another, and from the air a slow river may look like a snake wriggling its way along. In Greece there was a slow river called the Meander, and you will hear it said today and in our country that a stream meanders. It will mosey, which is an American way of saying that it meanders.

Linked up with wander in the word wanderlust is a word that has acquired a bad reputation through no fault of its own. The

German word lust was first used to express pleasure and delight. A little later it was used to tell of a man's appetite and desire. Possibly man's appetite and desire got too strong, so strong that they changed the meaning of the word. Lust came to mean uncontrolled desire and it began to be used in such bad words as bloodlust.

In wanderlust, however, lust is cheek by jowl with a word we all love, wander, and this is bound to improve its reputation and give it some of the meaning it had before it was spoiled. The word lusty, too, is a gentling of the word. Lusty means hearty — sometimes it means too hearty, perhaps, but it's a pleasant word just the same.

So the quintessence of wanderlust is right there in the word itself and deep down in all of us. It's a strong desire to move around and see what we can see for the sheer joy of it.

P.S. Considering how old is the desire to wander, it is strange that the word wanderlust is one of the new words in the English language. It came into use in the early 1900's. It was about that time that people realized how easy it was to get on ships and see the world. They needed a word in everyday speech to describe the impulse to travel. For travel had become a pleasure. It has not always been. The word travel was originally spelled travail, a word that meant and still means hardship or hard labor, and people would speak of a journey as a travail. But moving around got easier and easier and the word began to be spelled travel and it became a romantic word, full of lure and encouraging wanderlust on a world scale.

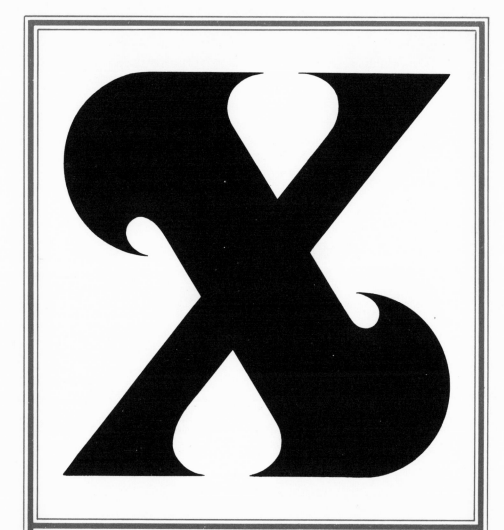

is for Xenophobia

X is for XENOPHOBIA

In the old days the world was bigger than it is now. That is, it took such a long time to get from one place to another that even a small part of the world seemed very large. People lived tightly together with their own kind and were suspicious of those they did not know or know to be their own kind.

Words sprang up to give names to this special kind of suspicion. One was from Roman days. It was the word foreign. To show you how closely Romans guarded their own little territories, foreign comes from the Latin word meaning door. Foris is the word. A foreigner was a person who was on the outside, out of doors. If he didn't belong inside the house or the gates of the city, he was a foreigner.

The Greeks had a word for it, too. Their word was xenos, which means stranger. And for good measure they added phobia to it from their word for fear, phobos, and made xenophobia, the fear of the strange or the foreign. We know about phobia because we hear people say they have a phobia about something, a deadly fear, one that is not reasonable. There are mental diseases that have phobia in them. There is claustrophobia, which is the fear of closed spaces (cloisters or closets). And there is agoraphobia, which is the fear of open spaces, the fear of great stretches of land or distances. And you have heard about hydrophobia. This is now called rabies. But not long ago it was noted that a mad dog would not drink water. People saw this and said it was because he was afraid of water. Hydro is from the Greek word for water. So the dog was said to have hydrophobia.

All peoples seem to have had an unreasoning fear of people who were not familiar (that is, not of their own families). The Hebrews had it, and there is one passage in the Old Testament that tells how they used a word to tell whether people were of their kind. The people of Gilead were attacked by the people of Ephraim. The attack failed and the Ephraimites sought to get away. They were so much like the Gileadites that they were almost able to escape. But it was known that the Ephraimites could not pronounce the word shibboleth. They said sibboleth instead. In this way and by this test the Ephraimites were sorted out and slain — forty-two thousand of them, the Bible tells us.

The fear of the foreign — xenophobia — continued right on down through history. People did not like those who were not like them. Even in Massachusetts Bay Colony in the early days of this country, a household or an inn was not allowed to keep a stranger unless his presence was reported to the authorities.

Have we got over this kind of fear, or, with the world shrunk, as men say, by faster ways of getting around, are there just more strangers? Well, this is the day of curtains, iron and bamboo, when people try to keep out ideas that are strange or foreign to their own way of thinking. It is the day of the Berlin Wall, built to keep people from getting to see other people.

Let us hope that some day both xenophobia and foreign will be marked arch. or obs. in the dictionaries. Arch. will tell us that they are archaic — from the Greek word meaning old. Obs. will mean that they are obsolete — from the Latin term meaning that they have gone out of use.

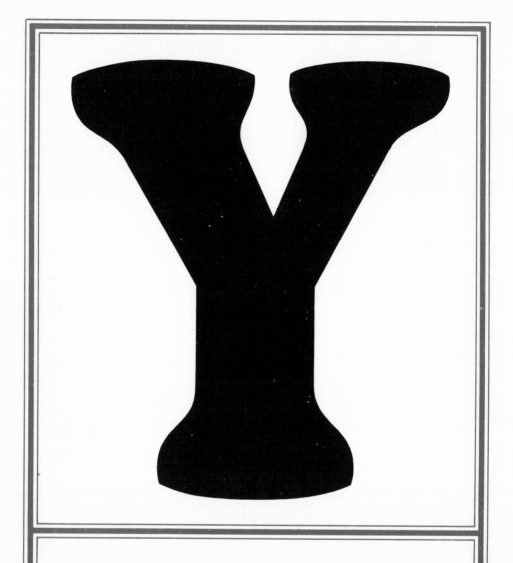

is for Yachtsmanship

Y is for YACHTSMANSHIP

Yacht is a Dutch word. Before we got hold of it in English and changed the spelling to suit us, the word was spelled jaghte. Considering how smooth, beautiful, racy and classy yachts are today, you'd hardly guess that they are descended from pirate ships. But that is what jaghtschips were in the old days when the Dutch had the run of the seas, when they were a great seafaring people and were at home upon the waters. They built a ship for pursuit, for the chase. The name they gave to it in Dutch (jaghte) meant hunter. It was light and fast and trim and could overtake almost any prey.

As the Dutch became more civilized, the jaghte passed to another use. It became a sporting vessel for dignitaries and was used on ceremonial occasions. Later still it became a vessel used for cruising, and then, as men learned to make sailing ships go faster and faster, the yacht was used almost entirely for racing.

So much for yachts and how they came to be in the first place and how they came to be what they are now. But in the word yachtsmanship you might say that we have a word with a ship on both ends and a man in the middle. What is the meaning of this? Especially what is the meaning of the ship at the end of the word — at what sailors would call the stern?

The ship in yachtsmanship has nothing to do with yachts or other kinds of ships. You find it in lots of words that have nothing to do with the sea, such as sportsmanship, lordship, championship, authorship, fellowship, craftsmanship, even hardship. A ship tacked onto the end of a word in this manner comes down to us from Old Teutonic and Old English words that meant to create or ordain or appoint. These old words are akin to our word shape. You might think of the ship at the end of yachtsmanship and sportsmanship, for examples, as shape rather than ship. A person skilled at sport has the shape of sport. It's our way of paying a compliment. Yachtsmanship (or yachtsmanshape) merely means that a man has the ability to handle a yacht, make it behave itself and go fast.

So you'd better think of ship — unless it's one that sails the seven seas — as simply a suffix, and you remember that a suffix is a sound or syllable at the end of a word that changes or adds to its meaning. When ship was fastened to such a word as yachtsman it just gave it added dignity, underlined it and made it broader.

The fact of the business is that the suffix ship has been tacked on to too many words and people are beginning to get tired of it. You can tell this by the way they make fun of it or use it in a humorous way. A British writer, Stephen Potter, has written some popular books on what he calls one-upmanship. He talks in a kidding way about the art of winning games without actually cheating but simply by flustering the other fellow and taking advantage of him. One-upmanship is amusing to read about because we have got sick of hearing people talk so much about sportsmanship and all the other ships besides the real ones.

But don't drop the suffix ship altogether. Just be wary of it and use it sparingly — with a little craftsmanship.

is for Zoological

Z is for ZOOLOGICAL

You may have heard the old ditty:

I went to the animal fair,
The birds and the beasts were there.
The old raccoon by the light of the moon
Was combing his auburn hair.
The monkey he got drunk
And ran up the elephant's trunk . . .

A good time was had by all, but especially by the fellow who went to the animal fair. Today an animal fair is called a zoological garden by men who manage it and know about animals. But most folks, who simply want to go out and ogle the animals, don't want to say all that much. About a hundred years ago British families got tired of saying of a Sunday, "Let's go out to the Zoological Gardens in Regent's Park." They decided to cut off most of the word and just leave the head. They said instead,

"Let's go to the zoo." And the word zoo got into the dictionaries.

The zoo draws people the way the sun draws plants. It attracts them, pulls them. Ever since antediluvian days people have been attracted by animals. You remember the story of Noah — how, when the Flood came, he was told to take two of every living thing of all flesh, male and female, to keep them alive.

Ancient kings and emperors used to keep animals on display. Sometimes they were cruel and beastly to the animals, as the Romans were, but at other times rich men and rulers around courts simply liked to look at animals and to study them.

Among the first people to study animals and get a knowledge of them were the Greeks, chiefly Aristotle, who died in 322 B.C. So it was logical that the Greeks should have given us the base of our word zoological. The Greek word for animal is zoion, and in our language it is turned into the prefix zoo in zoological and in dozens of other words that tell us something about what people call our dumb friends. Dumb meaning simply that they don't talk our language. No matter how big the word, if it begins with zoo or zo, you can count on its being an animal word.

You may find zo at the end of a word, also. You have heard or will hear sooner or later of the Paleozoic Age. That was long before the Flintstones, even. And Paleozoic tells in one word a story that took millions upon millions of years to happen, men of science say. Paleo comes from a Greek word meaning ancient and it is combined with zoic. By the zo we can guess that it pictures the age in which animals began to emerge out of elemental ooze and take shape upon the earth.

The number of words with zoo and zo in them tells us a lot about people and about how many ways people have thought about animals. The word zoolatry shows us that people have worshiped animals, that they are often tied in with religious belief. Some great religions, including the Hindu, believe that the soul may enter an animal after death and then come back and enter a human being again. It gives you pause to think about this and makes for zoophilism, which is a love of animals. You wouldn't step on an ant; it might be your great-grandmother. There probably has never existed any kind of animal that somebody didn't like.

It all goes to show how men from earliest days have been thinking that there is some kinship, some back-and-forthness, between men and animals. There is a lovely story among the old Greek myths about a giant with a hundred eyes. His name, Argus, has come down to us through the word Argus-eyed, meaning a person who can see everything or, as we say, has eyes in the back of his, or more likely her, head. When Argus was killed by Hermes it was said that his eyes were put in the handsome and glittering tail of the peacock. And that is how the peacock got all those brilliant spots.

Another zoo word that tells us a lot about people is zoomorphism. This means seeing things in animal shapes or forms. Long, long ago men of Babylonia noted that groups of stars had the look of animals, and the Babylonians began to name many of these groups after animals.

The Babylonians passed the idea on to the Greeks, who gave the name zodiac (literally an animal circle) to the twelve sections of the heavens where shapes could be seen at one time or another throughout the year. The Greeks also gave to the animal shapes names that we still use. One group of stars looked like a lion and they called it Leo; another resembled a scorpion and they called it Scorpio.

The ancients believed that these figures that appeared up there had some influence on humans at the time of their birth. Scientists do not believe this, but it is interesting to see how old beliefs survive in the language we use every day. The word disaster comes from the Greek word astron, meaning star. A disaster means that something has gone wrong with the stars and that a great misfortune has befallen the people of the earth as a result. Maybe nobody believes it but everybody says it when he speaks of a disaster.

You have to have a lot of imagination to find any of these animal shapes in the heavens. But the ancients had plenty of imagination, and so do most folks before they are, as Shelley puts it, "corrupted by the world's slow stain." There was the boy who told his mother that he had seen a lion in the street. She had seen the animal too and knew it was a collie dog with most of his body shaved for the summer. He had a mane like a lion.

"Go upstairs and ask the Lord's forgiveness for saying that," she told the boy.

He obeyed her, and when he came back she asked him if he had asked for forgiveness for a lie. He said yes. Then she asked him what the Lord said. "He said," the boy replied, "that when He first saw it, He thought it was a lion too."

Well, there we are — from A to Z, as we say, from A to Zed, as the English say. From Antediluvian to Zoological. We've come a long way, especially considering all the side roads we've taken.

And now we are right back where we started, for what have antediluvian and zoological in common? Animals, of course. Think of the Flood and we think of the Ark. You might even say it was the first zoo.

We didn't know that the A and Z in this book would be related. The fellow who wrote it didn't know it himself when he started. But that is one of the joys of writing.

Another joy is that the author always gets the last word. The only way you can get the last word is to write your own book. How about an alphabet book?

THANKS

Alphabet is a word that describes the order in which the speech sounds of a language are arranged so that they can be easily remembered. It comes from alpha and beta, the first two letters of the Greek alphabet. The order of letters differs in various languages, as you will see when you look up the table of alphabets in any good dictionary. Sometimes letters get shifted around — and for strange reasons. The letter z, which the British call zed, was sixth in the Greek order of letters. The Romans adopted the Greek alphabet but foolishly thought they could get along without z. By the time they found couldn't, the Roman alphabet was pretty well set, and when the Romans picked up z again there was no place to put it but at the end. We took our order of letters from the Romans and that is why z tags along where it is.

The study of alphabets is a quick way to get interested in the story of the human race. The development of speech sounds touches every phase of life. For example, the Egyptians had an alphabet of sorts fifty centuries ago, but they never did learn to trust words made up of letters alone. They felt, like some people today, that you had to have pictures to make meaning clear. When their word sef had the picture of a sun by it, the word meant yesterday; when it had the picture of a child by it, sef meant baby.

The Phoenicians got rid of that nonsense. They were business-men whose vessels plied the seas and they needed a language that was good for lists and bills and records. The result was an alphabet without pictures that served the purposes of trade — more or less as shorthand. There were no written vowels. You filled them in yourself, just as you know today how to fill out an abbreviation. You know what you say to yourself when you see Dr. or Mr. or Mt. or St.

Greece, not as big as Alabama but the most cultured country of Europe about thirteen hundred years before Christ, did busi-ness with the Phoenicians, and much of this business involved writing. The Phoenicians were great peddlers of papyrus, a material made from a huge swamp plant of the same name, and used for sails and writing materials. Later the word papyrus would be the root of our word paper. The Phoenicians fetched papyrus from Egypt and set up stores of it in their religious capital, the city of Byblos. So closely identified were papyrus and writing with Byblos that the Greek word for book was taken from the name of the center of the papyrus trade. The Greek word biblos and our word Bible are thus derived from a place name, just as in our day hamburger is named after Hamburg, Germany, and frankfurter is the name of a smoked sausage made first in another German city, Frankfurt.

The Greeks saw that the Phoenicians had a good thing in the alphabet and they latched on to the idea and adapted it to their own tastes and needs. For one thing, they added vowels to their alphabet. They liked the sounds of language written down to be remembered.

You will find the story of alphabets in books. One book you may enjoy particularly is *The 26 Letters* by Oscar Ogg. Writing as a calligrapher (there we have kalos and graph again), he unfolds a fascinating story, partly because he loves the beauty of old handwriting but also because he knows and shows how important language is to history.

Various dictionaries tell the story of words, but one you will find especially helpful as you go on learning more and more about language. It is *The Oxford English Dictionary*. In its full form (thirteen huge volumes) it is somewhat unhandy to have around the house. But there is a useful condensed version in two volumes, *The Shorter Oxford English Dictionary*. Those who compiled the *O.E.D.* took seventy years to comb English writing from the time of King Alfred and record how each word was used at a particular time. In this way we are able through the *O.E.D.* to tell when a word came into the language and how its meaning may change. Look up the word manage and trace it from its first use in 1561 and you will see the value of the *O.E.D.* and how much the history of a single word tells you about people.

And people in turn will tell you something about language every day. Years ago young friends of mine, the Roy Schaubs, taught their two-year-old daughter Dena the word hippopotamus. Dena loved it, bearing out the conviction voiced by Dr. Samuel Johnson: "Babies do not want to hear about babies; they like to read about giants and castles."

Later a lad named David Barclay Plaisted asked the meaning

of the word estuary in a way that suggested that he liked the sound and mystery of it. The question about estuary and Dena's liking for hippopotamus made it seem natural to put a lot of impressions together in the form this book took, using a polysyllabic word for each character in our alphabet.

Once started, of course, I needed help — all I could get from books and then some. I asked Professor Steele Commager of Harvard University to give me the benefit of his knowledge of Greek and Latin. He graciously agreed and, in fact, vetted the manuscript, as the British would say — the word meaning to scrutinize and coming from the practice of having a veterinarian go over an animal very carefully. It needs hardly to be added that Professor Commager caught errors that would have been a disgrace in a book of this sort. And if others are left, they are in material added since he saw the manuscript.

Next I asked Eva H. Grant, editor of the *P.T.A. Magazine*, for counsel and comment on the project, knowing her lively interest in the way reading is taught and in the way it should be taught. Her comment was both cordial and helpful, particularly in the advice on the choice and character of words to be included and in suggesting that quotations from literature illustrating the use of the big words be added wherever possible.

Margaret Barns, a trained librarian and teacher, gave her experienced view of the manuscript, made valuable comments and corrections, and tried out some of the material by reading it to children. So did Fred W. Herron and Fulton Oursler, Jr., associates of mine, and Elizabeth Atkinson Plaisted, an avid, prodigious, and omnivorous reader, who is of invaluable aid to me in research.

You can see that friends and Phoenicians alike have had a vital part in the making of the book. Two other associates must be mentioned. Caroline Rogers helped find instances of the way the words for which the letters stand are used in speech and writing; and Sidney Gordon, with a British background in theater and journalism, read the manuscript and caught mistakes that would have amused the British.

Perhaps the greatest help came from the publishers, Little, Brown and Company, notably Larned G. Bradford, editor in chief, and J. Randall Williams, senior vice-president, for they were undeterred by neophobia and showed a quick willingness to publish the book in a day when the paradigm is big pictures and little words.

CHARLES W. FERGUSON

This book was designed and decorated
by John Alcorn.
It was set in 12 point Bookman by
Cecil H. Wrightson, printed by offset
at Quinn & Boden on Warren's 70 lb.
#1854 Regular Offset, and bound in
G.S.B. S/535 Sun Gold bookcloth at the
Quinn & Boden bindery.